D1315899

WORLD LEADERS

STEWART ROSS

Thomson Learning
New York

WORLD LEADERS

Books in this series:

Propaganda
Victims of War
Women's War
World Leaders

Cover illustration: A 1939 poster showing Hitler and Stalin, soon to be on opposite sides, jogging along in an uneasy alliance.

First published in the
United States in 1993 by
Thomson Learning
115 Fifth Avenue, NY 10003

First published in 1993 by
Wayland (Publishers) Ltd.

Cataloging-in-Publication Data applied for

ISBN: 1-56847-079-7

Printed in Italy

Picture acknowledgments
The publishers would like to thank the following for permission to use their photographs in this book: Arkiv für Kunst und Geschichte/Image Select *cover*, 13, 23; Camera Press 8, 10, 20, 30, 31; Imperial War Museum 4, 11, 12, 14 bottom, 18, 21, 22, 27, 28, 29, 32, 34, 37, 40, 41; Popperfoto 9, 16, 19, 42; Topham/Associated Press 6, 14 top, 35, 36, 38, 39; Wayland Picture Library 5, 7, 43.

Contents

Dictators and democrats

The era of World War II threw up a number of remarkable war leaders. Some, such as Germany's Adolf Hitler and the USSR's Joseph Stalin, were dictators who appeared to exercise almost complete personal control over their countries. Other leaders, including Britain's Winston Churchill and the United States President Franklin Delano Roosevelt, headed democratic states. They too were very powerful, with far more authority than they would have had in peace time.

World War II can be seen as a struggle

The Allies' three most important leaders: (left to right) Joseph Stalin of the USSR, Franklin D. Roosevelt of the United States, and Winston Churchill of Britain meeting in Tehran, 1943.

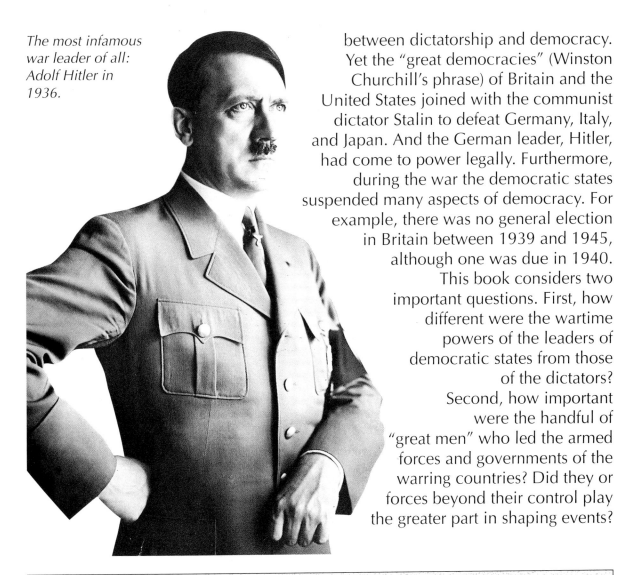

The most infamous war leader of all: Adolf Hitler in 1936.

between dictatorship and democracy. Yet the "great democracies" (Winston Churchill's phrase) of Britain and the United States joined with the communist dictator Stalin to defeat Germany, Italy, and Japan. And the German leader, Hitler, had come to power legally. Furthermore, during the war the democratic states suspended many aspects of democracy. For example, there was no general election in Britain between 1939 and 1945, although one was due in 1940.

This book considers two important questions. First, how different were the wartime powers of the leaders of democratic states from those of the dictators?

Second, how important were the handful of "great men" who led the armed forces and governments of the warring countries? Did they or forces beyond their control play the greater part in shaping events?

The historian A. J. P. Taylor was quite sure how important the major war leaders were: *Essentially only the political leaders counted. It is hardly an exaggeration to say that four men – Hitler, Churchill, Roosevelt, and Stalin – made every important decision of the war personally. (The Second World War.)*

Other historians are less sure of the importance of individuals. They have suggested that without the backing of other powerful forces, leaders could not have had as much influence as they did. Hitler, for example, was backed in his bid for power in Germany by a powerful and wealthy group of industrialists, without whom he could not have become German leader.

Adolf Hitler
(1889–1945)

> *We are all convinced . . . that he* [Hitler]
> *is the mouthpiece and pathbreaker of the*
> *future. Therefore we believe in him.*
> *Beyond his human form, we can see . . .*
> *the active grace of destiny.*
> (Joseph Goebbels, *The Goebbels*
> *Diaries 1939-1941*)
> *Pastor Dietrich Bonhoeffer, a descendant*
> *of eminent Protestant clergymen on both*
> *sides of his family . . . regarded Hitler as*
> *Antichrist and . . . believed it a Christian*
> *duty to "eliminate him."* **(William L.**
> **Shirer, *The Rise and Fall of the Third Reich*.)**

Probably no man in this century aroused such strong emotions in people as Adolf Hitler. No world leader was so fascinating or was believed to have had so much influence on events. His controversial personality dominated the era of World War II.

Born in Austria, Hitler fought for Germany in World War I. Like many Germans, in 1918 he felt bitter that the German armies had surrendered without being defeated. He believed they had been "stabbed in the back" by the politicians.

After the war Hitler became a politician. He was an energetic member of the extreme right wing National Socialist (Nazi) party. During the 1920s the Nazis made little headway. But the world economic crisis which began in 1929 brought severe hardship to millions of Germans, persuading many of them to look to the Nazis for salvation. Hitler shared the rising discontent with the Weimar Republic (see panel) and understood the popular desire for law and order. In the March 1932 presidential elections he received 30 percent of the votes. Four months later the Nazis were the largest single party in the *Reichstag* (German parliament), although they did not have an overall majority. On January 30, 1933 Hitler was made chancellor of Germany by the President, Von Hindenburg.

German troops surrendering in World War I. Hitler carefully exploited the humiliation felt by many Germans at the surrender of their undefeated armies in 1918.

Germany's crisis
Germany faced a double crisis in the early 1930s.
1. The Weimar Republic, the political system set up after Germany's defeat in World War I, was unable to provide stable government.
2. Much of Germany's recovery after the war depended on money borrowed from the United States. After the 1929 Wall Street Crash many U.S. financiers demanded their money back, bankrupting German businesses and causing high unemployment (1928: 1 million unemployed; 1933: over 6 million).

Hitler's Nazis announced that they were the last hope for a desperate people.

Hitler speaking at a public meeting. In the 1930s his brilliant speeches at huge, carefully managed rallies attracted many Germans to the Nazi cause.

Hitler was a brilliant and ruthless politician. Once the Nazis were in power, they were determined never to give it up. Guided by Hitler, they forced through an Enabling Act (March 1933), which gave Hitler special authority to deal with Germany's crisis. By 1936 most opposition had been eliminated, and the Nazis had seized control of the army and declared Hitler "Führer [leader] of the German Reich." The Nazi government began spending millions of marks on rearmaments and public works, such as the famous autobahn superhighways, and the economy started to recover. Hitler's declared aim, set out in his book *Mein Kampf* (My struggle), was to make the Germans the "master race" of Europe.

The 1919 Treaty of Versailles, drawn up after World War I, imposed very harsh terms on Germany. As well as having to pay heavy reparations, Germany lost much territory inhabited by German-speaking peoples. Hitler made no secret of the fact that he wanted to take this land back. On March 7, 1936, Hitler sent German troops into the demilitarized zone of the Rhineland. Although ordered to return if they were opposed, the troops met with no resistance. Two years later, having come to agreements with Japan and Italy, Hitler again ignored the Treaty of Versailles by uniting Germany and Austria.

In September 1938 Hitler prepared to invade Sudetenland in western Czechoslovakia, which had a large German population. A European war seemed imminent. But at a meeting at Munich on September 29, Hitler persuaded the British and French Prime Ministers, Chamberlain and Daladier, that Sudetenland was his "last territorial ambition," and he was allowed to go ahead with his occupation. After the occupation of the rest of Czechoslovakia in March 1939, Britain guaranteed the independence of Hitler's next target, Poland. Having negotiated a nonaggression pact with the USSR on August 23, on September 1, 1939 Hitler's forces invaded Poland. Britain and France declared war on Germany two days later.

German light tanks entering Poland, September 1939. Britain and France had said that they would not allow Poland to be invaded: when Hitler ordered his troops to invade, Britain and France declared war on Germany.

A starving inmate of a Nazi concentration camp. Hitler carefully made
sure he was not directly associated with such atrocities.

Did Hitler want war?
Some scholars believe that Hitler's foreign policy risked war, but did not plan for it. They say that *Mein Kampf* was propaganda, and that he advanced step by step, deciding on his next move only when he saw how things stood. They argue that, after what he had seen at Munich, he thought that Britain and France would not intervene when he invaded Poland. Other experts say that all along Hitler followed the aggressive foreign policy he had sketched out in *Mein Kampf*, knowing it was bound to lead to war.

In 1938 Hitler had removed the German army commanders who disagreed with his policies. After the outbreak of war he devoted himself to military matters, taking complete command on December 19, 1941. This meant that individuals within the Third Reich such as Heinrich Himmler (police chief and minister of the interior) and Air Force Commander Hermann Goering were able to build up huge personal power.

The most dreadful aspect of Nazi government was the persecution of the Jews, which in 1941 became an attempt to wipe them out completely. Hitler had fed German anti-Semitism, issued anti-Jewish laws, and helped establish concentration camps. He certainly knew and approved of the terrible sufferings of the Jewish people. Perhaps fearing for his reputation, Hitler left the detailed arrangements of the concentration camps to others.

Hitler's ability as a military commander is uncertain. He supported the successful tactics of *blitzkrieg* (lightning war)–a term he first used at a Nazi rally in 1935–which allowed his armies to sweep across Western Europe in 1940. On June 22, 1941, Hitler's forces made a surprise attack on the USSR. At first the armies made rapid progress, but by the winter their advance had been halted by a Soviet counterattack. Hitler's decision not to allow a German retreat at this point may have saved his armies from destruction by the advancing Soviets. Throughout the war his leadership is believed to have inspired German troops to remarkable acts of bravery: General Rommel noted, "At the Führer's command they were ready to sacrifice themselves to the last man." It was partly to prevent this from happening that Rommel joined a plot to assassinate Hitler in July 1944.

On the other hand, Hitler rarely visited the battle fronts, leaving him out of touch with military reality. In May 1940, when the Allied armies were at his mercy, for some reason he did not order his tank divisions to move in for the kill. This allowed the bulk of the British Army to flounder home from Dunkirk. Later, particularly in North Africa, Italy, and the USSR, Hitler's

On April 29, 1945 Hitler married his female companion Eva Braun. Before they committed suicide the next day, Hitler defended his career in a *Political Testament*: I have been actuated solely by love and loyalty to my people . . . It is untrue that I, or anyone else in Germany, wanted the war in 1939 . . . I die with a happy heart, aware of the immeasurable deeds... of our soldiers at the front . . . That from the bottom of my heart I express my thanks to you all is just as self evident as my wish that you should ...on no account give up the struggle...against the enemies of the Fatherland.

Uneasy friendship: Hitler greets Erwin Rommel, the brilliant general who finally joined a plot to assassinate him in 1944.

refusal to allow his forces to withdraw tied the hands of the field commanders and led to pointless loss of life. His 1944 Ardennes offensive (the Battle of the Bulge) was costly and stood little chance of success, and his decision never to surrender led to ghastly slaughter and destruction in Germany during 1945.

Since 1945 millions of words have been written about Hitler. Some accounts emphasize his abilities, others play them down, saying that he rose to power on a wave of German discontent as the political spokesman of German industrialists. Hitler has been criticized as a bungler who, had he listened to sensible advice, might have made his dreams of a "Thousand-Year Reich" come true. Others believe that it was not his talents that enabled him to achieve so much power, but the weakness of those who opposed him, both within Germany and in other countries.

Had he lived in a different country during a different age, Hitler might have achieved nothing. But he was born into circumstances that allowed his ideas to spread and his policies to be carried out.

A face in the crowd? A famous 1914 photograph of the declaration of World War I shows the young Hitler as just one of a huge crowd.

Benito Mussolini (1883–1945)

Mussolini was the first fascist dictator to come to power. He was also the least tyrannical, but in the end the most ridiculous. Invited by the King of Italy to become prime minister in 1922, he gradually set up a one-party state. By 1929 his Fascist Council had replaced the cabinet, and from then until 1943 Mussolini was the supreme authority in Italian politics. His government emphasized obedience to the leader, public works, pride in the Italian state, and the virtues of war. The regime was supported by brilliant propaganda campaigns, which built up a heroic image of the country's *Duce* (leader).

Mussolini believed in war as a way of uniting people and bringing glory to the Italian state. "Fascism," he said in 1932, "believes neither in the possibility nor the utility [usefulness] of perpetual peace." This attitude was

Mussolini's fascism

The *Fascist Program* of 1922 was typical of Mussolini's vague, emotional appeals to all groups of people: *Fascists, Italians! The hour of the decisive battle has come . . . Fascism* [does not] *march against the members of the public administration, but against a class of imbecile and weak-minded politicians . . . The* [middle class] *knows that fascism wishes to give aid to all those forces which advance its economic expansion and well-being. The working class . . . have nothing to fear from fascism. Their just rights will be loyally preserved . . . We call upon Almighty God . . . to witness that only one impulse moves us, only one desire unites us: to contribute to the salvation and to the greatness of our country.*

Fascist propaganda shows Mussolini's face imprinted on the map of Rome. The message: Mussolini represents the whole of Italy and its capital, Rome.

all very well when Mussolini bullied weaker states. But unsuccessful involvement in World War II brought the fascist regime down and led to his death.

Involvement in World War II was Mussolini's fatal mistake. The war ruined Italy's economy and, partly as a result, was not popular at home. The Italian army and navy were heavily defeated. To make matters worse, the dictator declared war on the United States, sent troops to help Hitler in the USSR, and issued a string of unrealistic commands that his generals could not obey. By the end of 1941 Italy was almost entirely dependent on German military and economic aid.

Mussolini's health began to give way and he grew increasingly pessimistic about the chances of victory. The Allies invaded Sicily on July 10, 1943. A fortnight later *Il Duce* was forced to resign. Rescued from prison by a daring German raid in September, he headed a fascist regime in Northern Italy until April 1945, when he was captured and executed by his own countrymen.

Over the years Mussolini came to believe much of the exaggerated praise heaped upon him in fascist propaganda. Overshadowed by Hitler and always promising more than he could deliver, by 1940 Mussolini had become little but a "ludicrous legend." When he died five years later he was no longer a leader of any importance on the world scene.

In Milan, Italy, after execution, the bodies of Mussolini, his mistress Clara Petacci, and other prominent fascists were strung up by their heels in a gruesome gesture of humiliation.

Francisco Franco (1892–1975)

Franco spent his early life as a soldier in the Spanish army. Having distinguished himself fighting in Morocco (then a Spanish colony), in 1934 he became involved in politics when he broke up a group of communist miners in Spain. By 1936 Franco was chief of the general army staff and in position to play a key role in Spain's future.

Spain, which had become a republic in 1931, was a bitterly divided country. There were right-wing groups, such as the Catholic church, the army, wealthy landowners, monarchists, and the Spanish fascist party (*Falange*). Ranged against them, but suspicious of each other, were the numerous reforming and left-wing groups of the Popular Front. These included liberals, socialists, communists, and anarchists. The situation was further complicated by Basque and Catalan separatists from the north of the country, who wished to break away from Spain.

In February 1936 the Popular Front won the elections and formed a government. Alarmed by the success of the left and mounting violence, on July 18 Franco decided to move. He led an army revolt in Morocco and crossed to the mainland, appealing to all right-wing groups: "Spaniards! To whoever feels a holy love of Spain . . . to those who have sworn to defend Spain from her enemies, the nation calls you to her defense. Are we to abandon Spain to her enemies? . . . No!" Spain was plunged into years of civil war. Three months later the military named Franco as head of the Nationalist state.

A 1937 Spanish postcard illustration linking Franco with Hitler and Mussolini. During the Spanish Civil War Franco was happy to accept the support of fascists at home and abroad.

¡HEIL HITLER!

¡VIVA ESPAÑA!

¡VIVA L'ITALIA!

Franco (center) attending a funeral at the height of the Spanish Civil War (1937), which his action had begun the previous year. When World War II broke out in 1939, he refused to become actively involved.

The Spanish Civil War, July 1936–April 1939

In some ways the war was a dress rehearsal for World War II. Franco led a right-wing Nationalist coalition against a loose union of Republicans. The Nationalists eventually won because they were better led and armed, and because they received important support from Hitler and Mussolini. Almost 1 million people died in the conflict.

1936: Nationalists move to the mainland. With German and Italian assistance, by the end of the year Franco controls half of Spain. The Republicans are helped by the USSR and International Brigades of volunteers.

1937: Franco fails to take the center of Spain but defeats the Basques in the northwest. German air power used to devastating effect, notably on the town of Guernica.

1938: Republican-held area cut in two and their offensive defeated.

1939: Franco takes Madrid and Barcelona. War ends.

After the Civil War the Nationalist government of Franco, *el Caudillo* (the leader), was recognized by the major democratic powers. He strengthened his position by building up the Falange (fascist) party, the only party allowed in Spain, and organizing the country along the lines of Mussolini's Italy. Franco knew that the Spanish were tired of war, and he refused to be drawn into the Axis alliance. On October 23, 1940 he met Hitler at Hendaye in France to discuss a possible alliance. To Hitler's frustration, Franco proved one of the few world leaders whom he could not overawe and Spain remained neutral. Franco did not necessarily reject Hitler's fascism. He probably saw his policy as the only realistic one for a nation too divided and exhausted by years of civil war to fight any more.

After the war, despite condemnation by the victorious Allies, Franco held his independent line. In 1947 he declared that he would remain *el Caudillo* for life. However, as he grew older he gradually made his regime more liberal. After Franco's death in 1975, Prince Juan Carlos became king.

Neville Chamberlain (1869–1940)

British Prime Minister Neville Chamberlain has often been blamed, perhaps unfairly, for a tragic lack of political judgment. Of all the anti-fascist leaders in power during the 1930s, he has been most strongly criticized for not taking a strong stand against the ambitions of Nazi Germany. Yet he belonged to a generation that had witnessed the slaughter of millions of young men in World War I and for whom another war was almost unthinkable. At least until 1939 Chamberlain was not out of touch with popular opinion–he represented it.

Chamberlain became prime minister of Britain's National Government on May 28, 1937. He had proved a conscientious and hard-working politician. But he lacked experience in foreign affairs, which made it difficult for him to handle the tricky international situation. Until March 1939, when Hitler occupied the Czechoslovakian capital of Prague, Chamberlain followed a policy of appeasement (see box on the next page). He did not act when Hitler

Appeasement

The policy Chamberlain's policy of appeasement, which had widespread support in Britain until 1939, meant avoiding war by talking with Hitler face-to-face and giving way to his demands.

The defense • Remembering the horrors of 1914-18, almost anything was better than another large war. • Communism, which promised worldwide revolution, was more to be feared than the Nazis–a strong Germany would act as a buffer against the communist USSR. • Until 1939, the British people would not have supported another European war. • Protected by the Royal Navy and the Maginot Line, Britain and France felt safe from a Nazi attack. • The longer war was delayed, the better, as Britain needed time to rearm. • Germany had been harshly treated by the 1919 Treaty of Versailles–Hitler's aggression was therefore understandable and, to some extent, justifiable.

The criticism • Appeasement made Britain look weak and encouraged Hitler to make more and more demands. • Chamberlain paid more attention to his personal advisers than to the warnings of the Foreign Office. • Britain had a duty to support the small democracies of Eastern Europe.

broke the Treaty of Versailles and united Germany with Austria in 1938.

Later in the same year Chamberlain gave way to Hitler's demands for the Sudetenland in Czechoslovakia and returned home to announce, "I believe it is peace for our time." After meeting Hitler at Munich he said of the fascist dictator, "I got the impression that here was a man who could be relied upon when he had given his word." History proved Chamberlain wrong.

When he saw how mistaken he had been, the prime minister guaranteed Poland's independence and finally went to war when Hitler invaded that country on September 1, 1939. But even at this late stage Chamberlain had tried to get the Poles to give way to Hitler's demands, and his unsuccessful efforts to make an alliance with the USSR were at best half-hearted.

Ill and depressed, Chamberlain resigned as prime minister on May 10, 1940. He remained in the government until just before his death in November.

Dead soldiers of World War I. Politicians such as Chamberlain remembered the numbers that had died and preferred almost anything to another war.

Winston Churchill (1874–1965)

When Britain went to war in 1939 Winston Churchill was sixty-five years old. He had been a soldier, journalist, writer, and politician, but he had not held government office since 1929. Many thought his career was over.

During the 1930s Churchill had campaigned on two issues. One was his determination to preserve the British Empire in the face of calls for independence. The other was his unfashionable opposition to the fascist dictators and his demands for British rearmament. In recognition of this, on the outbreak of war Prime Minister Chamberlain appointed him First Lord of the Admiralty, a post he had held from 1911 to 1915.

On May 10, 1940, as (in Churchill's words) an "avalanche of fire and steel" rolled westward toward the Channel, Chamberlain resigned. Senior politicians

---

Churchill and Appeasement

Churchill was one of the few British politicians who resolutely opposed Chamberlain's policy of appeasing Hitler and Mussolini. At the time his speeches seemed narrow-minded, especially to those who saw communism as a greater threat: 1934: *I dread the day when the means of threatening the heart of the British Empire should pass into the hands of the present rulers of Germany…I dread that day, but it is not perhaps far distant.* 1938: [The Munich agreement was] *only the first sip, the first foretaste of a bitter cup which will be proffered to us year by year, unless…we arise again and take our stand for freedom as in the olden times.*

Churchill at a weapons test in 1940. Pictures such as this were used to portray Churchill as a determined fighter who would never give in to his enemies.

agreed that Churchill's hour had come, and he was made prime minister.

Churchill's coalition government lasted until July 1945. As prime minister and minister of defense, Churchill had many powers. The War Cabinet gave him control over every detail of the war effort. Even the men commanding the armed forces, the chiefs of staff, generally went along with his ideas. He summed up his powers thus: "All I wanted was compliance with my wishes after discussion." On occasion Churchill faced opposition in parliament, most notably in July 1942 when the Germans sank 21 of the 34 ships on a convoy to the USSR. Nevertheless, his position was never seriously threatened; the British people were unable to vote for or against his government in an election until 1945, although one should have been held in 1940. In the influence he wielded and the way in which the media built up an image of him as an infallible chief, Churchill was not unlike the totalitarian leaders. Rarely in modern British history had so much power been

Churchill's oratory
In the end Churchill's reputation rested to a great extent on his ability to capture–and even mold–the mood of the British people. Never was this more plain than in his speeches of 1940. On May 13, in an effort to prepare the British people for the hardships ahead, he told the House of Commons:
I would say to the House . . . I have nothing to offer but blood, toil, tears and sweat. . . . you ask, What is our aim? I can answer in one word: Victory–victory at all costs, victory in spite of all terror, victory however long and hard the road may be; for without victory there is no survival.

Churchill just before broadcasting the news that Hitler's Germany had been defeated, in May 1945. Five years before, his brilliant radio speeches had been the single most important factor in convincing Britain that defeat was not inevitable.

On June 18, in what was probably his most famous speech, he was most concerned with raising morale: *I expect that the Battle of Britain is about to begin. Upon this battle depends the survival of Christian civilization . . . if we fail, then the whole world . . . will sink into the abyss of a new dark age . . . . Let us therefore brace ourselves to our duty, and so bear ourselves that, if the British Empire and its Commonwealth last for a thousand years, men will say, "This was their finest hour."*

One German general reckoned Churchill's leadership was worth thirty armored divisions.

concentrated in the hands of one person.

Although no one denies Churchill's remarkable contribution to his country's war effort, he did make strategic misjudgments. He may have overestimated the ability of massive bombing raids to damage Germany's industrial production in 1942-43. His insistence on sending convoys to Russia, many of which sustained very heavy losses, wasted precious resources. And his belief, shared by many others, that Japan would not be drawn into the war meant that Britain was ill prepared for a land war in the Far East.

On the other hand, Churchill understood that Britain could not possibly win the war alone. He surprised many people in the way he warmly accepted the Soviet Union as an ally after Hitler attacked it in June 1941. Churchill worked even harder for United States support. Many of his speeches were aimed at U.S. as well as British audiences. He enjoyed a close friendship with President Roosevelt, whose country remained neutral until December 1941. The relationship resulted in the U.S.

Churchill the actor. Like many war leaders, Churchill had a strong sense of theater and loved showing off before crowds. He made his bowed stance, cigar, and two-fingered victory sign symbols of his country's will to fight.

To many observers the defeat of Churchill's Conservative Party was a shock. But the British people had had enough of foreign affairs and felt that Labour offered better prospects for post-war social and economic recovery. Churchill was understandably upset by their decision, but he did not lose his good humor. When his wife Clementine suggested that the result might well be a blessing in disguise, he observed wryly, "At the moment it seems quite effectively disguised."

Lend-Lease Act of March 1941 (enabling Britain to borrow $10 billion of U.S. aid by 1945) and a joint declaration of peace aims, known as the Atlantic Charter (August 1941).

In the end Churchill's success in forging an alliance of the United States, the USSR, and Britain undermined his international position. In 1943 he had persuaded the U.S. to participate in a Mediterranean campaign which led to invasion of Sicily and Italy, and he was influential at the conference in Tehran between the USSR, the United States, and Britain (November-December 1943), which was held to discuss conduct of the war and the arrangement of the post-war world. But by 1944, as the might of Soviet and U.S. forces began to make itself felt, Britain had become the third and least powerful member of the Allied coalition. Despite Churchill's presence at the Yalta Conference of February 1945, it was clear that, in future, power would lie with the United States and USSR. Churchill attended the Potsdam Conference of July 1945, but had to leave after his government lost the British general election.

With the labour victory in 1945, Churchill became leader of the opposition. His speech at Fulton, Missouri, on March 5, 1946, in which he declared that, "an iron curtain has descended across the Continent," can be said to mark the start of bad relations between the United States and USSR. Churchill was prime minister again from 1951-1955.

Victorious Labour politicians who defeated Churchill's Conservatives in 1945. After the war, people voted for a new government in the hope that the war's end would bring a change for the better to everyone.

Joseph Stalin (1879–1953)

When war broke out in Europe in September 1939, Stalin, secretary of the Soviet Communist Party, had been the supreme authority in the USSR for about ten years. During this period his ruthless rule had both helped and hindered the USSR in preparing for World War II.

Based on government production targets set in three Five-Year Plans (1928-32, 1933-37, and 1938-42), Soviet industry made enormous advances. Steel production rose from 4 to about 20 million tons, coal from 31 to about 180 million tons, and oil from 11.7 to about 34 million tons. Many of the new factories were sited in the east of the country, away from the vulnerable western border. By the time of the Nazi attack in 1941, the USSR was a major world industrial power, capable of producing enough tanks, aircraft, and other weapons to wage war successfully against the Germans.

There was another, far less attractive side to Stalin's government. His fear of all opposition led Stalin to frequent "purges" of the Communist Party, the armed forces, government officials, and other potentially troublesome groups. Political commissars and the secret police spied on all officers and soldiers, eliminating anyone even vaguely associated with anti-Stalinist views.

Stalin became aware of the threat posed by Nazi Germany before any Western leader. But because he was a totalitarian communist, whose regime was hated and feared by men such as Chamberlain, Stalin was

Stalin's Red Army in 1941
Although massive, at the outbreak of war the Red (Soviet) Army had serious weaknesses.
1. 10,000 officers had been purged, leaving the army seriously short of experienced commanders.
2. Stalin, who at this stage had little military understanding, interfered in every aspect of his forces' operations.
3. The soldiers were poorly trained and much equipment was either lacking (e.g. radios) or largely out of date (e.g. tanks).

The Nazi-Soviet Pact, August 1939

Background Alarmed by the anti-Russian statements in *Mein Kampf* and the rapid German rearmament under Hitler, Stalin feared that, in time, the Nazis would try to expand German territory into the USSR. • Poland and the Western democracies refused to commit themselves to an alliance with the USSR. • In 1939 the USSR's industry and armed forces were not ready for war with so powerful a country as Germany.

The Pact Negotiated by foreign ministers Ribbentrop (Germany) and Molotov (USSR), the pact said:
• Neither country would attack the other or support the other's enemies. • (Secret clause) Eastern Europe would be divided between Nazi and Soviet spheres of influence.

Results • Hitler was free to invade Poland. • Stalin bought time to prepare for a possible war with Germany. • There was a chance, Stalin believed, that the nations of Western Europe would fight each other to a standstill, leaving the USSR the dominant power on the continent.

unable to persuade them to take his warnings seriously. During the 1930s there were three dominant types of government in Europe: democracy, fascism, and communism. They were all suspicious of each other, but before 1939 most democratic leaders feared communism more than fascism.

Isolated from other European states, Stalin went his own way. He made treaties with neighboring countries, such as the Baltic states and Czechoslovakia. On a more practical level, he sent military assistance to the Chinese fighting the Japanese and to the Republicans in the Spanish Civil War. After the Czechoslovakian crisis of 1938 Stalin was desperate to stall the coming German attack and agreed to the Nazi-Soviet Non-Aggression Pact of August 23, 1939.

Stalin's role during the war is not easy to judge. He insisted on overseeing every aspect of the Soviet forces. He undermined the army's morale with political arrests and executions, and he was certainly not a great commander. But he gradually learned to trust and support men more skilled than himself, such as Red

A Soviet purge committee at work, 1933. The purges of people suspected of opposing Stalin deprived the USSR of many of its most able citizens.

Army Commander Zhukov, and they brought the USSR the victories it needed. His drive helped the modernization and reequipment of Soviet forces, although they never matched the Germans for efficiency. At crucial moments, as in June 1941 and the assault on Moscow at the end of the year, he lost control of events. Overall, however, he provided the Soviet people with a focus for their dogged resistance.

Stalin was suspicious of his British and U.S. allies because he knew they disliked communism. He was particularly annoyed that they did not invade Western Europe before 1944. At one stage he even tried to persuade them to open up a "second front" by hinting that he might come to a separate agreement with Hitler. At the Tehran, Yalta, and Potsdam conferences Stalin proved a tough negotiator. His great fear was that after the defeat of fascism the Western Allies would turn their might against an isolated and exhausted USSR.

Both during and after the war Stalin did all he could to ensure that never again would his country be invaded from the west. He had taken the first steps even before the defeat of Germany, often refusing to support noncommunist resistance movements. By 1949, communist governments, backed by Soviet

Russian soldiers taken prisoner by the German armies that invaded Russia in June 1941. Stalin was so shocked by the speed and success of the German invasion that he remained in drunken isolation for days. He reappeared full of determination and energy.

troops, were set up in the countries occupied by the Red Army: East Germany, Poland, Czechoslovakia, Hungary, Romania, Albania, and Bulgaria. In 1949 COMECON was formed to bind these countries together economically. (Although communist, former Yugoslavia never came wholly under Soviet influence.) Many Western observers said that the establishment of a Soviet bloc in Eastern Europe was an example of Stalin's aggression. It can be argued that the Soviet leader's behavior was defensive, that he was only trying to defend his regime against threats from the democracies. The United States was far wealthier than the USSR and after 1947 it poured economic aid into Europe to support friendly governments. Moreover, the U.S. had the atomic bomb, a weapon not possessed by the USSR until 1949. We may ask ourselves whether the West was partly to blame for the mistrust that led to the era of conflict between the two superpowers.

A 1938 French cartoon showing what the democratic West thought of Stalin's totalitarian regime–the placard reads, "We are truly happy." The figure on the left is a Russian worker; the man holding a gun on him is Stalin. Three years later Stalin had become the West's most powerful ally. Soon after the end of the World War II, West and the USSR were in conflict again.

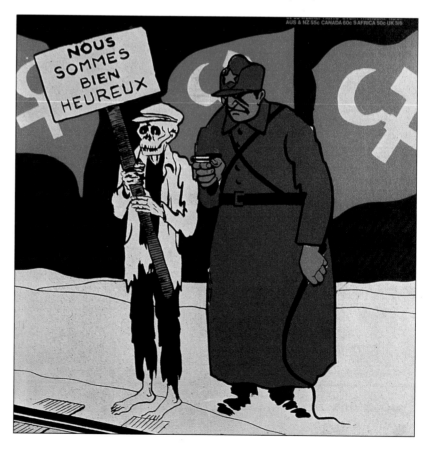

Hirohito (1901–1989)

From 1926 to 1945 Japan was theoretically ruled by Emperor Hirohito. In fact he was really only a symbol. Real power rested with industrial combines and the party of the extreme nationalists (the *Toseiha*), who had close links with the army.

Hirohito's position was a strange one. As emperor he was regarded by most Japanese as a divine figure, whose word could not be challenged. All laws and commands went out in his name. He attended cabinet meetings, although he generally kept quiet because he was supposed to be above politics. Army officers were pledged to absolute obedience to the emperor. One reason why they fought on for so long against hopeless odds in 1945 was that they did not wish to disgrace their emperor or reduce his status. Yet Hirohito had never been eager to pursue the war, and on August 15, 1945 he broke with tradition by using a radio broadcast to order his people to surrender.

The Japanese army, dominated by the *Toseiha*, became heavily

Emperor Hirohito on horseback. In theory, Hirohito was Japan's ruler.

The Japanese army and politics

The political importance of the Japanese army was based on • a strong traditional respect for the military; • the independence of all military matters from civilian control; • powerful reserve organizations; • compulsory civilian military training (1925); • the 1936 law that said that only a serving officer could be war minister; • the influence on civilian matters of the Imperial Headquarters, which was controlled by the army.

involved in politics in the 1920s. By the 1930s, as the political scene became more chaotic, the army had emerged as a stable and united force capable of directing policy. That policy included aggression toward neighboring states, and in 1931 Japan took over the Chinese province of Manchuria. Three years later it formed the Anti-Comintern (anti-communist) Pact with Nazi Germany. Full-scale war with China followed in 1937, and the plan for a Greater East Asia Co-Prosperity Sphere in 1938. Believing it was not his job to get involved in such decisions, Hirohito did not interfere.

A far more influential figure was General Hideki Tojo, the leading member of the Japanese militarist party. Having served in the army, Tojo became deputy war minister in 1938, war minister in 1940, and prime minister on October 14, 1941. From then until his resignation in July 1944 it was he, not the emperor, who dominated the Japanese government. Convinced that war with the United States was inevitable, he authorized the Pearl Harbor attack. Tojo then reorganized the

General Hideki Tojo, the most influential member of the Japanese wartime government. He failed in his attempt to commit suicide in 1945 and was executed by the Allies as a war criminal.

All that remained of the city of Hiroshima after an atomic bomb had been detonated above it. This awful destruction persuaded Hirohito that Japan would have to surrender.

Japanese administration controlling the country's new empire and appointed himself chief of staff in February 1944. After the war he was found guilty of war crimes and hanged, along with six other Japanese leaders.

Hirohito, the man for whom Tojo and his forces were supposed to be fighting, remained in the background, keeping his views to himself. He emerged only at the very end of the war. In 1945 he requested Tojo to seek a negotiated peace with the Americans before Japan was crushed. Finally convinced by the dropping of an atomic bomb on Hiroshima that surrender was the only course left open to his people, Hirohito formally submitted to the United States.

Following the Japanese surrender the Allies were not quite sure what to do with Hirohito. The Chinese, Australians, and New Zealanders wanted him put on trial for war crimes. The United States decided against this, believing the emperor would be a valuable right-wing force for stability in post-war Japan. So after he had admitted he was not a god, he was allowed to keep his title.

Hirohito remained a controversial figure for the rest of his life. Many Allied war veterans thought it was a disgrace that he was allowed to make a state visit to Britain in 1971. They said that although the emperor might not have been personally responsible for Japanese acts of aggression and apparent barbarity, he had the power to stop them but did not use it. Others argued that he had never been a political figure and could not be held responsible for what had been done in his name. The question is: can people be blamed for not doing what others think they should have done?

Emperor Hirohito on a visit to London. As the Japanese head of state, Hirohito visited Europe in 1971. Although the visit was criticized by some Allied war veterans, it helped reestablish good relations between Britain and Japan.

Chiang Kai-shek (1887–1975)

Chiang Kai-shek was president of China through-out the era of World War II. But his country was divided between the Communists and Chiang's Nationalists, and was partly occupied by the Japanese. As a result the president never had the sort of influence one might expect of the leader of the country with the largest population in the world. Following the overthrow of the imperial government in the revolution of 1911, China entered a long period of domestic strife. After the death of the revolutionary leader Sun Yat-sen in 1925, General Chiang rapidly built up his power. By 1928 he was the most powerful man in the country. He was president, commander-in-chief of the army, and chairman of the ruling *Kuomintang* (Nationalist) party.

Chiang's presidency was troubled from the beginning. The deeply corrupt *Kuomintang* was never very popular with the peasant classes, who made up most of the population. Party members diverted government funds into their own pockets, showed no real interest in democracy, and made little effort to improve people's lives. The army was unreliable too, rebelling in 1930, 1933, and 1936.

From 1931, when the Japanese occupied the province of Manchuria, Chiang also had to contend with invaders. To make matters worse, he was never able to come to a lasting peace with the Chinese Communists. In 1931 the Communists established a Chinese Soviet Republic in Kiangsi province, and there was a civil war until 1936.

Open war with Japan in 1937 brought the Chinese Nationalists and Communists into temporary alliance. Their efforts were not enough to stop the Japanese advance, and by the end of 1938 the invaders held the whole of China's eastern coastline. Chiang was forced to move his headquarters farther inland.

The outbreak of World War II brought Chiang new hope. He joined officially with the Allies on December 9, 1941. After Pearl Harbor he received plentiful American aid and in 1943 he was regarded as important enough to meet Roosevelt and Churchill at the Cairo Conference. During the previous year U.S.

Chiang Kai-shek (left) meeting President Roosevelt and Prime Minister Churchill on equal terms in Cairo in 1943. Although Chiang was theoretically head of one of the mightiest nations on earth, the Allies found him a disappointing ally.

Chiang Kai-shek at the age of 87, shortly before his death. Although ruler of the island of Taiwan, he insisted to the end that he was in fact President of the whole of China.

General Joseph Stilwell had been sent to China to advise Chiang in his struggle against the Japanese. Chiang and Stilwell (who soon recognized the president's military incompetence and offended him with the nickname Peanut) did not get along. Stilwell was called home in 1944. In 1945 Chiang's forces regained some territory from the Japanese, but by then the war was almost over.

With the withdrawal of Japanese troops from China, almost at once the Communists and Nationalists resumed their old hostilities. For a while the United States backed Chiang and tried to mediate between him and the Communist leaders Mao Tse-tung and Chou En-lai. But after January 1947 they left Chiang to fend for himself.

The end for Chiang was not long in coming. The Communists received widespread popular support and rapidly drove the Nationalists back to the sea. Peking fell in January 1949, and later that year Chiang fled to the island of Formosa (Taiwan). He stayed there for the remaining twenty-five years of his life, dreaming in vain of one day returning to the country of which he still believed himself to be president.

Chiang's career may suggest that individuals influence the course of events only when they are in tune with forces more powerful than themselves. This might help to explain why Mao succeeded where Chiang failed.

Mao Tse-tung
Mao was Chiang's most determined opponent. In 1934-35 he and other leaders saved the Communist army from the Nationalists by leading it on the famous 6,000-mile Long March to the northern Shensi province. He put the experience he gained fighting the Japanese in alliance with the Nationalists (1937-1945) to good effect in the ensuing civil war. In 1949 he became Chairman of the People's Republic of China. Unlike Chiang, Mao recognized the peasantry as the key to power in China, and in response to his promises of land and justice they flocked to him.

Franklin D. Roosevelt (1882–1945)

"This," said Nazi leader Goebbels when he heard of the death of President Roosevelt on April 12, 1945, "is the turning point." Of course Goebbels was wrong. Roosevelt was replaced as president by Harry S Truman and the United States fought on. But Goebbels and many others believed that Roosevelt was personally responsible for the way his country conducted the war.

Roosevelt was first elected President of the United States in November 1932, taking up office the following year. He offered the American people a "New Deal" to lift them out of economic depression, and during the early years of his presidency much of his time was taken up with domestic matters. His policies seemed to work and he was reelected in 1936.

Pearl Harbor

The surprise Japanese air attack on the U.S. Pacific naval base at Pearl Harbor on December 7, 1941 ("a date that will live in infamy" – Roosevelt) destroyed 19 U.S. vessels and 120 aircraft and killed 2,400 people. Congress declared war on Japan the next day. Critics of Roosevelt's administration have argued that his staff should have seen the attack coming and done more to defend against it. It has also been argued that some members of the government secretly wanted a show of Japanese aggression against the United States as a way of persuading the American people to back U.S. entry into the war.

Roosevelt being sworn in as President of the United States in 1941 for an unequalled third term of office. To win the 1940 election, he had played down his willingness for the United States to join World War II.

In Roosevelt's campaign for a third term as President, he had told the American people what they wanted to hear: "Your boys will not be sent to any foreign wars." But in 1939 he had stated, "When peace has been broken anywhere, the peace of all countries everywhere is in danger," and he did not really believe that the United States could stand and watch as Germany won control of the Atlantic and Japan the Pacific. His attitude was based on two viewpoints: the nation had a moral duty to uphold democracy, and it would be endangered if much of the rest of the world fell into the hands of dictators. Thus, while remaining officially neutral, he encouraged the build-up of the U.S. fleet and did what he could to assist Britain and to contain the Japanese. He swapped fifty old U.S. destroyers for the use of British naval bases in the Caribbean and the Atlantic, stepped up aid through the Lend-Lease Act of March 1941, and allowed the U.S. Navy to escort convoys most of the way across the Atlantic. In July 1941, alarmed at Japan's aggression in the Far East (particularly in China) and its fascist links, he froze all Japanese funds in the United States and later insisted that talks with the Japanese would have to be conducted on his own terms. Diplomatic negotiations were in progress when news of the Japanese attack on Pearl Harbor came through.

The Watts Bar Dam on the Tennessee River, built in 1942. President Roosevelt had initiated a federal economic recovery package, known as the New Deal, in 1933.

The President's Powers
American government operates within a written Constitution first drawn up in 1787. Two key principles underlie central administration: the separation of powers, and checks and balances. In theory these mean that policy is the responsibility of the President and lawmaking the job of Congress. The two institutions are quite separate and have ways of limiting each other's powers. (e.g. Congress makes laws, but they have to be signed by the President to become valid.) One result of this is that the President's power in foreign affairs is much greater than in domestic issues. Although Congress declares war, the President is Commander-in-Chief of the armed forces, appoints all ambassadors, and controls U.S. foreign policy.

American neutrality

Britain and her allies found America's unwillingness to enter the struggle against fascism hard to understand. They failed to recognize that U.S. politicians saw themselves as part of the New World, whose people rejected the squabbles of the Old World as having nothing directly to do with them. The famous aviator Charles Lindbergh expressed this view most forcibly when he said in April 1941, "We in this country have a right to think of the welfare of America first . . . If we concentrate on our defenses and build up the strength that this nation should maintain, no foreign army will ever attempt to land on American shores." Only the sneak attack on Pearl Harbor and Hitler's declaration of war four days later convinced American neutrals that it was now impossible for their country to stay out of the war.

Those who support Roosevelt's management of U.S. affairs during the war praise three things. First, the efficient way in which he used his country's industrial might to create a gigantic war machine capable of upholding its allies and grinding down its enemies. Second, his demand, often against the wishes of the military, that cooperation among the Allies was more important than doing what was immediately best for the United States. And third, his insistence that the war was a crusade for "four essential freedoms: freedom of speech and expression . . . freedom of every person to worship God in his own way . . . freedom from want . . . [and] freedom from fear."

Roosevelt's love of freedom and justice made him a champion of the idea of an international organization to oversee the post-war world. In August 1941, while the United States was still at peace, he joined with Churchill in producing the Atlantic Charter, outlining eight "global principles" for international understanding and

Roosevelt giving Churchill's famous "V-for-Victory" sign. After Pearl Harbor the friendship between the two men probably gave Britain more influence in world affairs than it had had before.

cooperation. These were adopted by twenty-six countries, which signed the United Nations Declaration at the President's official residence, the White House, on January 1, 1942. In San Francisco in 1945 the United Nations Charter was signed. In some ways it is Roosevelt's most enduring monument.

Throughout his long presidency Roosevelt had plenty of critics. They believed that he did not have a clear or realistic grasp of the overall world picture. He was too trusting of Stalin, they said, and overestimated the power of Chiang Kai-shek's Nationalists. (After 1945 the USSR seized Eastern Europe and Chiang was driven from China.) The President's opponents in Congress and the armed forces accused him of prolonging the war by insisting on unconditional surrender of the Axis powers and by backing plans to invade northern Europe over the Channel rather than push north from the Mediterranean.

Nevertheless Roosevelt inspired deep respect and love. When he died of a sudden stroke less than a month before Germany's surrender, American troops at the battlefront wept openly. (Described in Hugh Brogan's *History of the United States of America*.)

Roosevelt and Churchill, who were good friends, at a press conference in Casablanca, January 1943.

Roosevelt and Stalin

Roosevelt, the elected leader of the world's largest democracy, and Stalin, the communist dictator, made strange allies. For a long time Roosevelt believed that the USSR's suspicious attitude was partly the result of the way the Western democracies had treated the country before 1941. He had recognized the USSR in 1933 and during the war sought to break down Stalin's reserve by treating him as a trusted friend. This did not make Stalin any easier to deal with. Perhaps Roosevelt was too much of an idealist, or perhaps he was right when he confessed, "I don't know a good Russian from a bad Russian . . . I don't understand the Russians."

Harry S Truman (1884–1972)

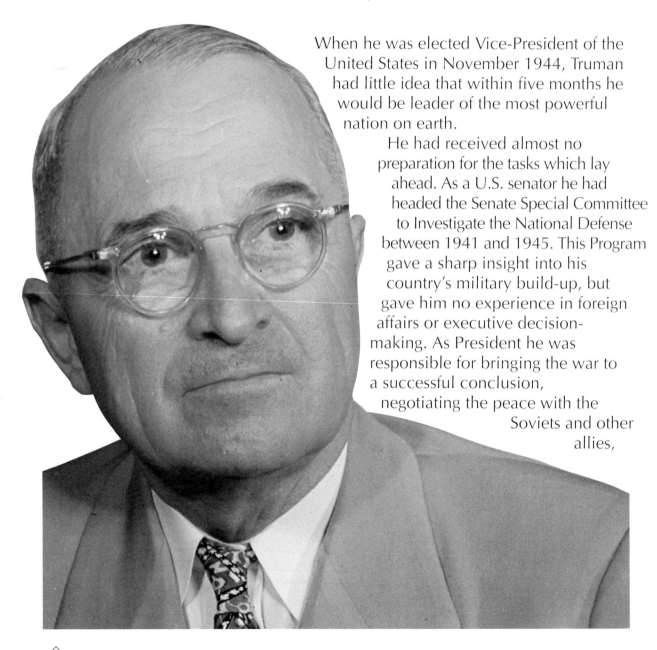

When he was elected Vice-President of the United States in November 1944, Truman had little idea that within five months he would be leader of the most powerful nation on earth.

He had received almost no preparation for the tasks which lay ahead. As a U.S. senator he had headed the Senate Special Committee to Investigate the National Defense between 1941 and 1945. This Program gave a sharp insight into his country's military build-up, but gave him no experience in foreign affairs or executive decision-making. As President he was responsible for bringing the war to a successful conclusion, negotiating the peace with the Soviets and other allies,

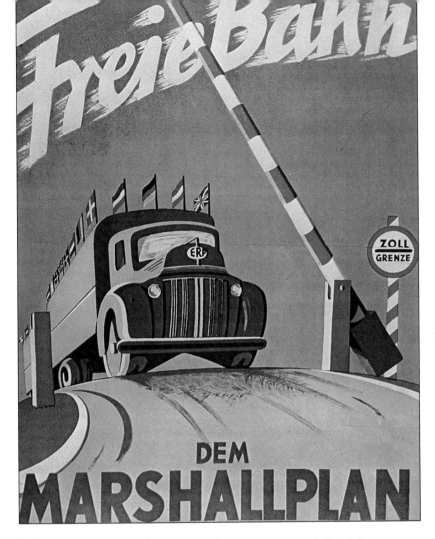

FreieBahn

ZOLL
GRENZE

DEM
MARSHALLPLAN

The Truman Doctrine
Truman set out his new foreign policy in a speech to Congress on March 12, 1947:
I believe that it must be the policy of the United States to support free peoples who are resisting attempted subjugation by armed minorities or by outside pressures. I believe that we must assist free peoples to work out their own destinies in their own way.

A German poster advertising the Marshall Plan, an offshoot of the Truman Doctrine. Under the terms of the Plan the United States gave the states of Western Europe $17 billion to speed their recovery from the war.

helping to set up the United Nations, and deciding whether or not to use the atomic bomb. To many people's surprise, Truman adapted to his new job very easily.

Truman delayed the start of the Allied Potsdam Conference (July 17, 1945) until after the successful testing of an atomic bomb. He hoped it would give him an extra bargaining counter in his discussions with Stalin. As it turned out, since they were not prepared to fight their old ally, the United States could do little about the presence of Soviet troops in most of Eastern Europe. Nevertheless, the Potsdam discussions seemed amicable enough, and there were not many obvious signs of the future rift between the two superpowers.

The decision to use the atomic bomb to bring the war against Japan to a swift end was entirely Truman's.

Many scientists said that the weapon was too terrible to be used. Military advisers, on the other hand, urged that unless the weapon was used the war would drag on for months, resulting in terrible loss of American life. The president was convinced by their arguments, and atomic explosions destroyed the cities of Hiroshima (August 6) and Nagasaki (August 9). Japan surrendered five days later. We still ask ourselves: did Truman make the right decision?

By the end of 1946 Truman was sure that it had not been enough for the United States to win the war–the peace must be won as well. By that he meant resisting the expansion of communism, "primarily through economic and financial aid." The Truman Doctrine meant that for the first time the United States would become actively involved as a global power in peacetime. It was, as he said, "a turning point in American foreign policy."

Although Truman said that he wished to support "free peoples," it can be argued that what he was doing was building up a network of states friendly to the United States. In other words, his policy was as much about defending U.S. interests as those of the countries he assisted. That is certainly how the Soviets saw it.

The inside of what had been a school in Nagasaki, destroyed by the atomic bomb dropped on the city in 1945. The decision to use this terrible weapon was made by Harry S Truman, then U.S. President.

Great men?

This book began with two questions. How different were the wartime powers wielded by the leaders of democratic states from those of the dictators? Did these war leaders really exercise as much influence as people have thought they did?

At the Tehran Conference of 1943, Stalin, Roosevelt, and Churchill met for dinner. During the meal the American adviser Harry L. Hopkins said light-heartedly, "The provisions of the British Constitution and the powers of the War Cabinet are just whatever Winston Churchill wants them to be." The Prime Minister rejected the comment, saying, "I was the only one of our trinity [Stalin, Roosevelt, and himself] who could at any moment be dismissed from power." He went on, "The President's term of office was fixed, and his powers not only as President but as Commander-in-Chief were almost absolute . . . [and] Stalin appeared to be, and at this moment certainly was, all-powerful in Russia."

Firefighters tackling a blaze after a bombing raid. Decisions made by wartime leaders affected the lives of millions and millions of people. Many of them died during the war, whether they came from democracies or dictatorships, through no choice of their own.

German troops moving into Holland, May 1940. It is inconceivable that any Dutch leader, however brilliant, could have saved the country from invasion.

It was actually very unlikely that Churchill would be fired. He had never been elected prime minister by the British people, and until an election was held Churchill was never really in danger of losing power (he did lose the election of 1945). The war had brought special circumstances in which all leaders were granted far more power than they would have had in peacetime. No leader lost power until the war was ending; Mussolini, Hitler, and Tojo died because their countries lost the war, and Churchill lost an election held after peace had been declared in Europe. In answer to the first question it could be said that although Hitler, and especially Stalin, held absolute power over their citizens, even the leaders of the democratic nations wielded extraordinary power during the war. Whatever the form of government in peacetime, in wartime the leader was allowed massive powers to conduct affairs effectively.

This brings us to our second question. Did the individual leaders really matter? Obviously, to some extent they did. When the advice of the generals and politicians had been taken, strategic decisions, such as that to drop the atomic bomb, had to be taken personally. Some would argue, however, that they should be seen only within a wider framework. For example, the British could expect to resist an invasion in 1940 only because they lived on an island and had a reasonable chance of surviving. Nothing could have saved the Dutch from the German tanks in May 1940. Similarly Hitler's leadership directed the German army to incredible feats of arms in 1939-41. But without Germany's desire to overcome the bitter humiliations of 1918-26 and without the backing of one of the most powerful economies in the world, his calls for a "Thousand-Year Reich" would have been so much hot air.

In history, individuals and greater forces are woven together in a tangle that we cannot ever hope to unravel completely. Therefore before we hasten to praise or blame the so-called "great leaders," it is worth bearing in mind the age-old saying: "Cometh the hour, cometh the man." You cannot have one without the other.

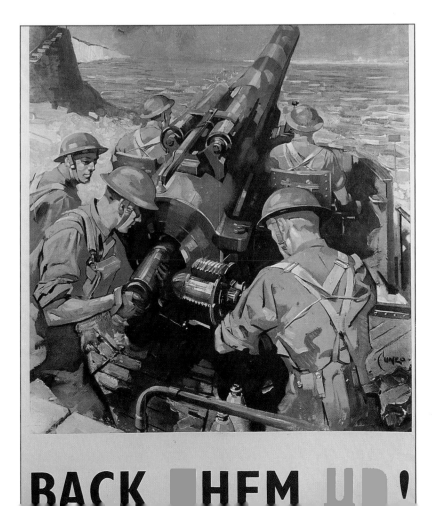

BACK THEM UP!

Opinion is divided about the extent to which World War II was influenced by "great men." This British propaganda poster of 1940 suggests that events would be decided not by individuals, but by the whole nation working together.

Glossary

Absolute   Having complete power.

Allies   The United States, Britain, and the other countries fighting the Axis powers.

Anschluss   Union, particularly that of Germany and Austria in 1938.

Anti-Commintern Pact   The agreement to resist the spread of communism made by Germany, Japan, and Italy in the 1930s.

Anti-Semitism   Hostility toward the Jewish people.

Armistice   A signed cease-fire.

Axis   The alliance of Germany, Italy, and Japan in the 1930s.

Blitzkrieg   Lightning War: the strategy of striking at the enemy hard and fast, using aircraft and armor.

Cabinet   The small group of leading government ministers.

Charismatic   Having a personality attractive to others.

Civil war   A war fought between people of a single country.

Coalition   A group formed by more than one party or country.

COMECON   Council on Mutual Economic Assistance formed in 1949 to aid countries in the Soviet bloc.

Communism   A political theory that all property should be held in common and there should be no private ownership of such things as factories and farms.

Concentration camp   A prison camp for specific groups of people–for example aliens or political opponents. In Nazi Germany millions of Jews and many other people were killed in such camps.

Constitutional monarchy   A form of government in which the monarch is head of state but has no political power.

Convoy   A number of ships sailing together.

D-Day   The code name for the Allied landings on the Normandy beaches, June 6, 1944.

Demilitarized zone   Territory where no troops or fortifications are permitted.

Democracy   Government by elected representatives of the people.

Depression   A severe economic slump. Depressions often involve high unemployment.

Dictatorship   Government by a single figure, the dictator.

Division   A large self-sufficient army unit.

Fascism   A totalitarian political system laying stress on nationalism and the figure of the leader.

Final Solution   The Nazi decision to exterminate all the Jewish people living within German-held territory.

Foreign policy   A country's policy toward other states.

Intelligence   The information a state's information-gathering service collects.

League of Nations   The unsuccessful international organization set up after World War I to preserve peace and develop cooperation among the countries of the world.

Left wing   Inclined toward socialism or communism.

Liberal   The political belief that stresses the rights and freedoms of the individual.

Maginot Line   A defensive line built 1929-34 in eastern France to defend against a possible German attack. In 1940 the Germans went around it by advancing through Belgium.

Mobilize   Prepare for war.

NATO   (The North Atlantic Treaty Organization) An anti-communist defensive alliance set up in 1949 by the United States and its European allies.

Neutral   Not taking sides.

New Deal   President Roosevelt's package of measures, introduced during the 1930s, intended to boost the U.S. economy. It involved the federal (national) government more closely in local affairs.

Occupy   Take over another territory, which is thereby occupied.

Offensive   A broad-ranging attack.

Purge   Get rid of supposedly unwanted or dangerous individuals.

Rearmament   Building up armed forces after a period of peace.

Reparations   Payments to meet the cost of the war. The payments are made by those who have been defeated.

Repression   The driving out of all opposition.

Republic   A state in which the head of government is an elected president and not a monarch.

Sanctions   Measures taken against a state, but not involving war.

Socialism   A political theory that all industry, capital, land, etc. should be in the hands of the state.

Totalitarianism   A political system that places all power directly in the hands of the state and its leader(s).

USSR   The Union of Soviet Socialist Republics–the communist state which replaced the Russian Empire after the 1917 revolution. The USSR was disbanded at the end of 1991.

Versailles, Treaty of   The treaty imposed on Germany after World War I.

Vichy France   The part of France that submitted to Germany in 1940 and was allowed a measure of self-government.

Books to read

Harris, Nathaniel. *Hitler.* North Pomfret, Vt.: Trafalgar, 1989.

Hoobler, Dorothy and Thomas Hoobler. *Showa: The Age of Hirohito.* New York: Walker & Co., 1990.

Italia, Bob. *Benito Mussolini.* Minneapolis: Abdo & Daughters, 1990.

Larsen, Rebecca. *Franklin D. Roosevelt: Man of Destiny.* New York: Franklin Watts, 1991.

Matthews, Rupert. *Winston Churchhill.* New York: Franklin Watts, 1989.

Sweeney, James B. *Army Leaders of World War II.* New York: Franklin Watts, 1984.

Whitelaw, Nancy. *Josef Stalin: From Peasant to Premier.* New York: Macmillan, 1992.

Chronology

1918	November 11	Armistice ends World War I.
1919	June 28	Treaty of Versailles signed.
1921	July 29	Hitler chairman of Nazi party.
1924		Hitler writes *Mein Kampf.*
1928		Stalin dominant in USSR.
1929	October 29	Wall Street Crash begins world economic depression.
1931		Japan takes over Chinese province of Manchuria.
	April 14	Spain becomes a republic.
1932	January 7	Germany stops paying war reparations.
1933	January 30	Hitler appointed chancellor of Germany.
	March 23	German Enabling Act.
	July 14	Nazis become the only legal party in Germany.
	August 2	Hitler made Führer.
1934	October	Civil violence in Spain.
1935	March 15	Germany openly rearming.
	October 2	Italian troops invade Ethiopia.
	October 19	Ineffective League of Nations sanctions on Italy.
1936	February	Left wins elections in Spain; civil violence.
	March 3	Britain increases defense expenditure.
	March 8	German troops enter Rhineland.
	July 18	Spanish Civil War begins.
	October 1	Franco head of state in Spain.
	November 1	Rome-Berlin Axis.
	November 18	Franco government recognized by Hitler and Mussolini.
	November 25	Italy joins Germany and Japan in Anti-Comintern Pact.
1937	April 27	German aircraft destroy Guernica during Spanish Civil War.
	July 7	Japan attacks China.
1938		Stalin's enemies being purged in USSR.
	February 4	Hitler becomes commander of all German armed forces.
	March 12	*Anschluss* (union) of Germany and Austria begins.
	August 12	German troops mobilize over Czechoslovakian crisis.
	September 27	Royal Navy mobilized.
	September 30	Czechoslovakian crisis defused at Munich Conference.
	October	Chiang Kai-shek's government moves to Chungking.
	October 1	German troops into Sudetenland.
1939	January 26	Franco's forces capture Barcelona.
	February 27	Britain and France recognize Franco's government.
	March 15	Czechoslovakia occupied by German troops.
	March 28	Franco's forces enter Madrid.
	March 31	Britain and France promise to uphold Polish independence.
	April 18	USSR suggests alliance with Britain and France.
	April 28	Hitler rejects peace proposals from President Roosevelt.
	May 22	Hitler and Mussolini's "Pact of Steel."
	August 23	Nazi-Soviet Non-Aggression Pact.
	September 1	Germany invades Poland.
	September 3	Britain and France declare war on Germany.
	September 17	Soviet troops into Poland.
	October 6	Hitler rejects peace moves by Britain and France.
	November 30	USSR invades Finland.

1940	April 9	Germans seize Norway and attack Denmark.
	May 10	German attack on Holland, France, and Belgium.
		Churchill replaces Chamberlain as prime minister.
	May 26	Beginning of Dunkirk evacuation.
	June	Soviet troops invade Baltic states.
		Battle of Britain begins (ends September).
	June 10	Mussolini declares war on Britain and France.
	June 22	France surrenders.
	September 14	Italy invades Egypt.
	September 27	Japan, Germany, and Italy form Tripartite Pact.
	October 28	Italy invades Greece.
	November 5	Roosevelt reelected President of the United Staes.
1941	February 9	German troops to North Africa.
	March 11	Lend-Lease Act signed.
	June 22	German invasion of the USSR.
	July	Embargoes on sale of oil and steel to Japan.
	August 7	Stalin supreme commander of Soviet forces.
	October 17	General Tojo prime minister of Japan.
	November	German forces halted outside Moscow.
	December 7	Japanese attack on Pearl Harbor.
	December 8	United States and Britain declare war on Japan.
	December 9	China declares war on Japan and Germany.
	December 11	Germany and Italy declare war on United States.
1942	January 20	Wannsee Conference proposes "Final Solution."
	February 15	Singapore falls to Japanese.
	May 4	Battle of Coral Sea (ends May 8).
	June 3	Battle of Midway (to June 6).
	July	Battle of Stalingrad begins (ends February 1943).
	October 23	Battle of El Alamein (ends November 4).
	November 11	Germans move into Vichy France.

1943	July 5	Beginning of Battle of Kursk (ends August 23).
	July 10	Allies land in Sicily.
	July 25	Mussolini resigns.
	September 3	Allies land in Italy.
	October 13	Italy declares war on Germany.
	November 28	Tehran Conference opens.
1944	March	Soviet troops into Poland.
	April 17	Fresh Japanese offensive in China.
	June 6	D-Day Allied landings in Normandy.
	June 23	Soviet offensive begins.
	July 18	General Tojo resigns as Japanese prime minister.
	August 21	Dumbarton Oaks Conference sets out framework for United Nations.
	October 6	Soviets into Czechoslovakia and Hungary.
	October 20	U.S. forces land in Philippines.
	November	Unrelenting bombing of Japan begins.
	December 16	Unsuccessful German offensive in Ardennes begins.
1945	February 4	Yalta Conference opens.
	April 1	U.S. forces land on Okinawa.
	April 12	Roosevelt dies – Truman becomes President of United States.
	April 20	Russians reach Berlin.
	May 7	Germany surrenders.
	June 26	United Nations formed.
	July 16	Potsdam Conference opens.
	August 6	Atomic bomb dropped on Hiroshima.
	August 8	USSR declares war on Japan.
	August 9	Atomic bomb dropped on Nagasaki.
	August 14	Japan surrenders.
	October	Civil war in China.
1946	March 5	Churchill's "Iron Curtain" speech.
1947	March 12	Truman Doctrine outlined.
	June 5	Marshall Plan put forward.
1948	June 24	Soviets begin blockade of West Berlin (ends May 12, 1949).
1949	January	COMECON established.
	April 4	NATO formed.

Index